CONTENTS

SO-EXE-366

CONTENTS

SONGS FOR THE YOUNG CHILD

SING and BE happy

VERSES
COMPOSED AND ADAPTED BY

Clara Belle Baker

FOLK MELODIES
HARMONIZED BY

Caroline Kohlsaat

SING AND BE HAPPY

Abingdon Edition, 1980

Library of Congress Catologing in Publication Data

Main entry under title:

Sing and be happy.
  1. Children's songs. 2. Folk-songs. I. Baker, Clara Belle. II. Kohlsaat, Caroline,
1875-
M1997.S6163 [M1627]   784.6'2406   80-13421

ISBN 0-687-38547-4

MANUFACTURED BY THE PARTHENON PRESS AT
NASHVILLE, TENNESSEE, UNITED STATES OF AMERICA

INTRODUCTION

It is hoped that *Sing and Be Happy* will be sung with joy by little children everywhere—in the home, in the church school, and in the weekday school.

The tunes have been chosen from folk songs having simplicity, charm, and beauty; they therefore are especially suited for the little child's singing. They are drawn from many nationalities: American, French, English, Swedish, German, Bohemian, Irish, Danish, Dutch, Lithuanian, Welsh, Russian, Syrian, Finnish, Sicilian. The folk melody, being complete in itself, may easily be sung without accompaniment. An accompaniment, if added, should merely serve the melody. The harmonizations in this book are in keeping with the simplicity and delicacy of the tunes. The child who can read music will enjoy playing the songs as well as singing them.

The songs are very short. In most instances, the form follows that of the original folk song, with the same rhyme scheme, the same phrasing, and a like simplicity. The subjects include nearly everything that surrounds the little child making life interesting and joyous. The child's relationship to the world is continually stressed, and for this reason the book is especially adapted for religious education. The child scatters crumbs for the birds, peanuts for the squirrels, gives milk to Pussy, bread to Bunny, takes good care of Mother, and plays with Baby. Valentines are made in February, and secrets are whispered at Christmas. The robin helps with the garden. The bee makes honey. The carpenter builds houses. The child's heart is filled with thankfulness.

> How great is God Almighty,
> Who has made all things well.

OUR PETS

Bow-Wow-Wow

CLARA BELLE BAKER

Bow - wow - wow! Come scam - per with me now. I'll chase the ducks in gras - sy nooks, And jump the fence and swim the brooks, And show you how, And show you how, And show you how, Bow - wow!

Pretty Pussy

CLARA BELLE BAKER

Pret - ty pus - sy, mew, mew, mew, I can guess what

troub - les you: You are ver - y tired of play - ing,

You are hun - gry, so you're say - ing. Pret - ty pus - sy,

mew, mew, mew, I'll soon have some milk for you.

The Bunny

CLARA BELLE BAKER

Bun - ny, pret - ty bun - ny, why raise your long ears? You

know me, lit - tle bun - ny, and what need for fears? I

give you green let - tuce and car - rots and bread, And

lit - tle house to live in with leaves for a bed.

Gold Fish

CLARA BELLE BAKER

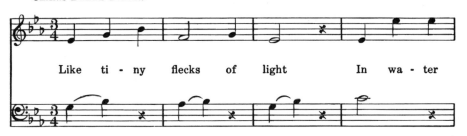

Like ti - ny flecks of light In wa - ter

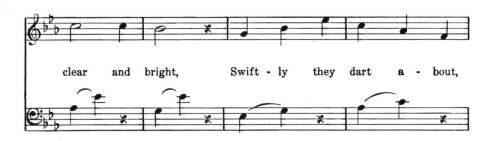

clear and bright, Swift - ly they dart a - bout,

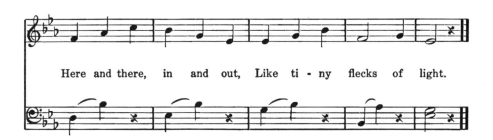

Here and there, in and out, Like ti - ny flecks of light.

6

Little Chickens

Hear them peep, peep, peep, Lit - tle chick - ens, lit - tle

chick - ens; Hear them peep, peep, peep; Un - der moth - er's wings they creep.

Snow Birds

Hear them tweet, tweet, tweet,
Little snow birds, little snow birds;
Hear them tweet, tweet, tweet;
Let us throw them crumbs to eat.

The Pony

Ride with me, my mas - ter, In the sun - ny wea - ther;

Down the hill and up a - gain We will go to-geth - er.

The Squirrel

CLARA BELLE BAKER

With bush - y tail and bright shin - ing eyes He

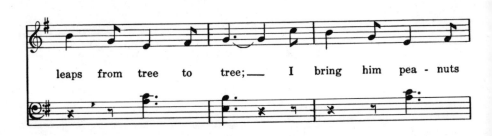

leaps from tree to tree;___ I bring him pea - nuts

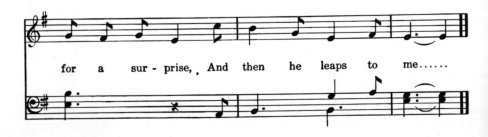

for a sur - prise, And then he leaps to me......

Lambkins and Shepherd

CLARA BELLE BAKER

Home from the green field where the brook is flow - ing,

Lamb - kins and shep - herd are to - geth - er go - ing;

In the warm fold all are creep - ing, Sheep and lambs no

lon - ger leap - ing; Soon they will be sleep - ing.

BIRDS, BEES AND BUTTERFLIES

Sing, Bluebird, Sing

CLARA BELLE BAKER

Sing, blue - bird, sing, And tell us it is

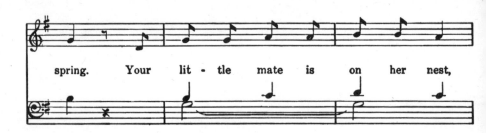

spring. Your lit - tle mate is on her nest,

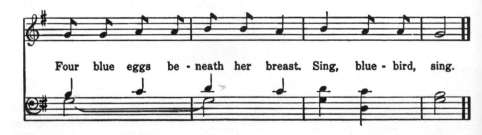

Four blue eggs be - neath her breast. Sing, blue - bird, sing.

The Woodpecker

CLARA BELLE BAKER

Black and white and flam - ing red, In the tree high o - ver - head, He is tap - ping all for fun, Rap - ping, tap - ping in the sun. Rap - tap - tap- tap, Rap - tap - tap - tap, Rap - tap - tap - tap, Rap - tap - tap - tap.

NOTE.—The woodpecker raps for four purposes: to make a home, to make a storehouse for nuts, to find insects, and to amuse himself. He is sometimes seen drumming on a resonant dead limb or a piece of tin roofing, solely "for fun."

Robin Redbreast

CLARA BELLE BAKER

Oh, I am Rob-in Red-breast, I hop on your lawn, I

help to make your gar - den, I wake you at dawn.

The Canary

Clara Belle Baker

I'm glad to see you here, Chee-ree-ree-cheer! Chee-ree-ree-cheer!

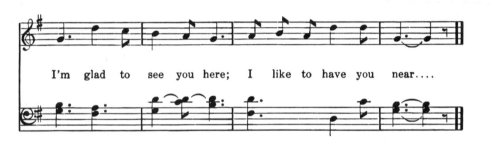

I'm glad to see you here; I like to have you near....

Singing

ROBERT LOUIS STEVENSON

Of speck-led eggs the bird-ie sings And nests a-mong the trees; The

sail-or sings of ropes and things In ships up-on the seas. The

chil-dren sing in far Jap-an, The chil-dren sing in Spain; The

or-gan with the or-gan man Is sing-ing in the rain.

The Bee

Clara Belle Baker

1. Hum, hum hum, Bee, I hear you come, Buz-zing, buz-zing,
in the flow - ers Through the sun - ny, sum - mer hours.
Hum, hum, hum, Bee, I hear you come.

2 Hum, hum, hum,
   Bee, I see you come,
   Bearing sweets that you have stolen,
   Sac of honey, bags of pollen.
   Hum, hum, hum,
   Bee, I see you come.

3 Hum, hum, hum,
   Bee, you still may come;
   For the honey that you gather
   I will eat with bread and butter.
   Hum, hum, hum,
   Bee, you still may come.

The Butterfly

CLARA BELLE BAKER

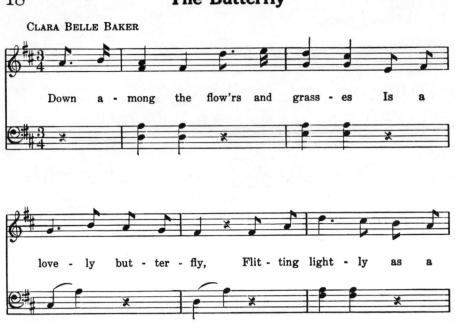

Down a - mong the flow'rs and grass - es Is a

love - ly but - ter - fly, Flit - ting light - ly as a

sun - beam, While the sum - mer hours pass by.

FLOWERS AND LEAVES

Dandelions

CLARA BELLE BAKER

1. When the first spring days are cold, Dan - de - li - ons, dan - de - li - ons, When the first spring days are cold, Dan - de - li - ons dress in gold.

2 When the summer days are bright,
Dandelions, dandelions,
When the summer days are bright,
Dandelions dress in white.

Bright-Eyed Daisies

CHRISTINA ROSSETTI

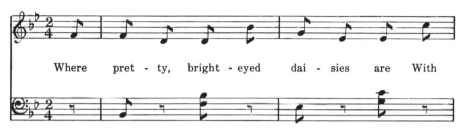

Where pret - ty, bright - eyed dai - sies are With

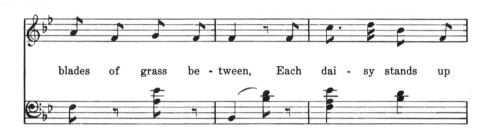

blades of grass be - tween, Each dai - sy stands up

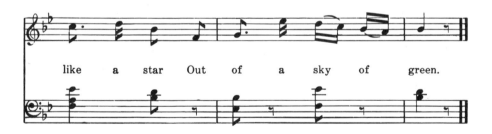

like a star Out of a sky of green.

Violet

CLARA BELLE BAKER

I am walk - ing through the grass, Vi - o - let!

And I pick you as I pass, Vi - o - let.

Pret - ty lit - tle flower of blue, Vi - o - let.

How the chil - dren all love you, Vi - o - let!

Pussy Willow

CLARA BELLE BAKER

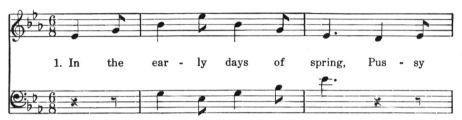

1. In the ear - ly days of spring, Pus - sy

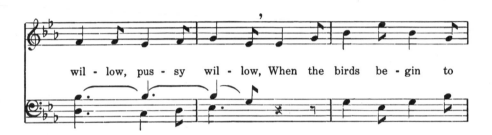

wil - low, pus - sy wil - low, When the birds be - gin to

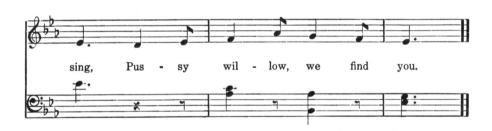

sing, Pus - sy wil - low, we find you.

2 And you wear a velvet gown,
Pussy willow, pussy willow,
That is soft as any down.
Pussy willow, we love you.

Gay Leaves

CLARA BELLE BAKER

Now the gay leaves on the trees,

Play - ing with the au - tumn breeze, Whirl - ing, twirl - ing

in the air, — Fall here and there. _____

Brown Leaves

CLARA BELLE BAKER

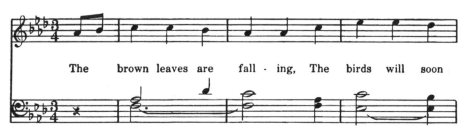

The brown leaves are fall - ing, The birds will soon

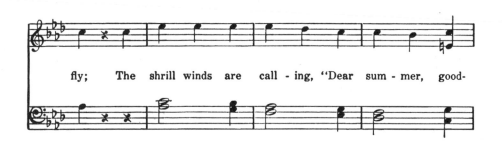

fly; The shrill winds are call - ing, "Dear sum - mer, good-

by, Dear sum - mer, good - by, good - by."

Seeds Fall

CLARA BELLE BAKER

Lit - tle seeds fall to the ground, Soft earth

cov - ers them from view, Snow-flakes form a cov - er

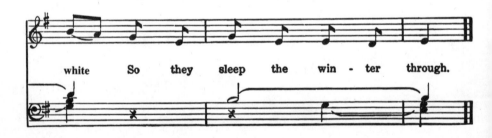

white So they sleep the win - ter through.

The Orchard

CLARA BELLE BAKER

1. If you go out to the or - chard,

You will find the blos - soms fair. Some are pink and

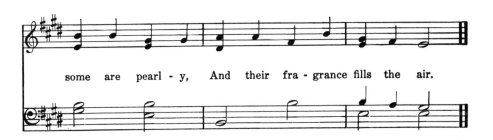

some are pearl - y, And their fra - grance fills the air.

2 If you go out to the orchard,

You will find the apples sweet.

Some are red, and some are yellow;

All are very good to eat.

WIND AND WEATHER

30 The Sun

CLARA BELLE BAKER

Good morn - ing to you, mer - ry sun, That shines bright all the
day; You watch the grass and flow - ers grow And
lit - tle chil - dren play; You watch the grass and
flow - ers grow And lit - tle chil - dren play.

Raindrops

CLARA BELLE BAKER

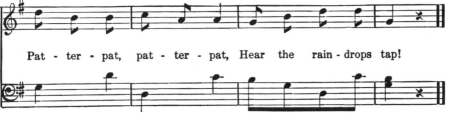

Moon and Clouds

CLARA BELLE BAKER

See the big round moon up high, Sail - ing, sail - ing in the sky. Now the dark clouds ri - ding o - ver Hide from view the love - ly ro - ver. Forth she bursts a - gain to sight, Sil - ver moon a - shin - ing bright.

Twinkle, Twinkle, Little Star

33

The Rainbow

CHRISTINA ROSSETTI

Boats sail on the riv - ers, And ships sail on the seas; But the
clouds that sail a - cross the sky Are pret-ti - er far than these. There are
brid - ges on the riv - ers As pret - ty as you please; But the
bow that brid - ges heav - en, And o - ver - tops the trees, And
builds a road from earth to sky, Is pret - ti - er far than these.

The Wild Wind

CLARA BELLE BAKER

Hear the wild wind whis - tle through the leaves, Woo - oo - oo;

FINE

Hear the wild wind whis - tle round the eaves, Woo - oo - oo;

D.C.

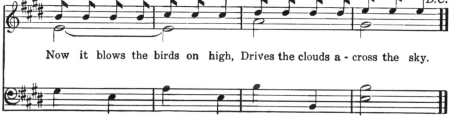

Now it blows the birds on high, Drives the clouds a - cross the sky.

Cold Nights

CLARA BELLE BAKER

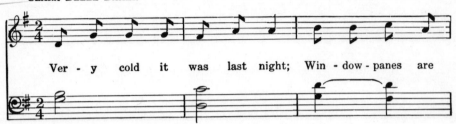

Ver - y cold it was last night; Win - dow - panes are

coat - ed white; Hoar - y frost lies all a - round

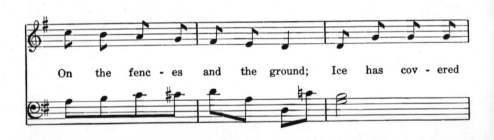

On the fenc - es and the ground; Ice has cov - ered

pond and stream, And my breath is turned to steam.

Jacky Frost

CLARA BELLE BAKER

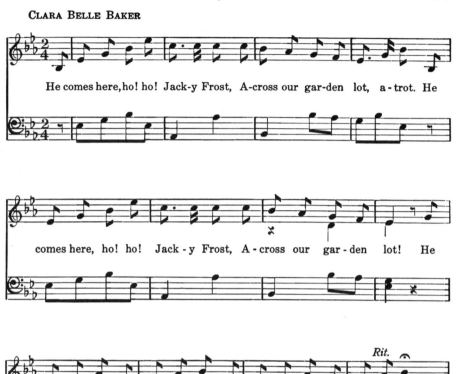

He comes here, ho! ho! Jack-y Frost, A-cross our gar-den lot, a-trot. He

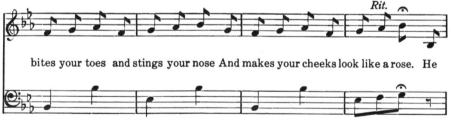

comes here, ho! ho! Jack - y Frost, A - cross our gar - den lot! He

Rit.

bites your toes and stings your nose And makes your cheeks look like a rose. He

comes here, ho! ho! Jack - y Frost, A - cross our gar - den lot!

Snowflakes

CLARA BELLE BAKER

Lit - tle snow-flakes, fall-ing light,   Drift a - cross the fields at night.

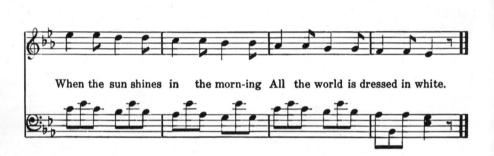

When the sun shines in   the morn-ing All the world is dressed in white.

Now It Is Spring

EDNA DEAN BAKER

Lo! cold win-ter days are past; Hark! rob-ins and or-i-oles sing;

Gay daf-fo-dils bloom at last, For now it is spring!

TRAVEL AND TRADE

42

Come A-Rowing

CLARA BELLE BAKER

1. Come a - row - ing, come a - row - ing, Where the wa - ters are a - flow - ing; Come a - row - ing, come a - row - ing In our gay lit - tle boat.

2 Come a-rowing, come a-rowing,
Where the lilies are a-blowing;
Come a-rowing, come a-rowing;
In the shadows we'll float.

The Airplane

CLARA BELLE BAKER

WECKERLIN

Most won - der - ful of ves - sels That sail a - cross the

sky of blue, That float a - mong the white clouds, Where

once the wild birds flew, —— Where on - ly wild birds flew, Most

won - der - ful of ves - sels, I'd like to sail with you.

44 Firemen

CLARA BELLE BAKER

Cling - a - ling - ling - ling! The gong is ring - ing! See the fire - men go - ing

to the fire! Hook and lad - der, hose and en - gine bring - ing,

See the fire - men go - ing to the fire! Now the en - gine stops!

Now the big hose drops! See the wa - ter stream-ing on the fire!

The Carpenter

45

CLARA BELLE BAKER

With a rap - a - tap - a - tap the car - pen - ter,

With a rap - a - tap - a - tap the car - pen - ter Builds

hous - es. With saw and plane and ham - mer bright

The car - pen - ter with all his might Builds hous - es.

Harvest Song

CLARA BELLE BAKER

1. Sing a song of wav-ing grain In the field,

Sing a song of wav-ing grain In the field.

Now we see the mow-ers all, Now the wav-ing grain will fall In the field.

2 Sing a song of bags of wheat
  In the mill,
 Sing a song of bags of wheat
  In the mill.
 Now the whirring wheels go round,
 Now the golden grain is ground
  In the mill.

3 Sing a song of snowy flour
  In the bin,
 Sing a song of snowy flour
  In the bin.
 Now we cut the biscuits out,
 Now the oven's piping hot;
  Put them in.

Trade Song

CLARA BELLE BAKER

1. The far-mer reaps the har - vest, The far - mer reaps the har - vest, The far - mer reaps the har - vest, While we go round a - bout, While we go round a - bout, While we go round a - bout, While we go round a - bout, — The far - mer reaps the har - vest, While we go round a - bout.

2 The baker bakes our biscuits.

3 The tailor makes our clothing.

4 The miner mines our silver.

PLAY AND REST

Children Playing

(All dance in circle)

In the spring, in the spring, Chil-dren play-ing, chil-dren play-ing,

In the spring, in the spring, Chil-dren play-ing laugh and sing.

(One child shows action)   *(All imitate)*

And they all do this way; Yes, they all do this way.

(Imitate)	1. Jumping rope	3. Bouncing balls
	2. Flying kites	4. Roller skating
	5. Hopscotch	

Did You Ever See a Lassie?

Old Game

Did you ev - er see a las - sie, a las - sie, a las - sie, Did you

ev - er see a las - sie do this way and that? Do

this way and that way, Do this way and that way; Did you

ev - er see a las - sie do this way and that?

NOTE.—The children stand in a ring. One child stands in the center while all sing the song. At the words, "Do this way," the child in the center shows any activity, such as hopping first on one foot, then on the other, washing clothes, etc., in rhythm to the end of the song. All the children immediately join in imitating the center child. She chooses a child to take her place and the game is repeated. When a boy is in the center "lassie" is changed to "laddie."

Swinging

CLARA BELLE BAKER

Up I go in-to the sun-ny air, When high and low I am swing-ing. I see the tall trees wav-ing ev-'ry-where, When high and low I am swing-ing. Now up toward the blue sky far a-way, Now down toward the earth where chil-dren play. How hap-py I am on a sun-ny day When high and low I am swing-ing!

The Little Elf

JOHN KENDRICK BANGS

1. I met a lit - tle elf man once Down

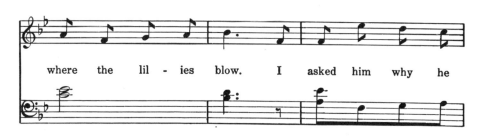

where the lil - ies blow. I asked him why he

was so small, And why he did not grow.

2 He slightly frowned and with his eye
   He looked me through and through.
"I'm quite as big for me," said he,
"As you are big for you."

NOTE.— The words are reprinted by permission from the St. Nicholas Magazine.

54   The Dolly

CLARA BELLE BAKER

1. I've a dear lit - tle dol - ly; She has

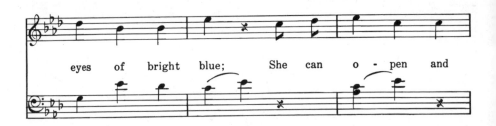

eyes of bright blue; She can o - pen and

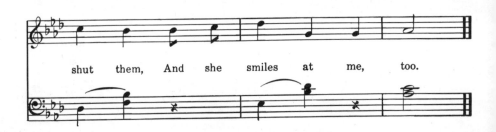

shut them, And she smiles at me, too.

2 In the morning I dress her,
And we go out to play;
But I like best to rock her
At the close of the day.

My Baby

CLARA BELLE BAKER

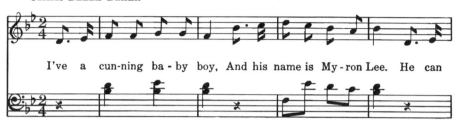

I've a cun-ning ba - by boy, And his name is My - ron Lee. He can

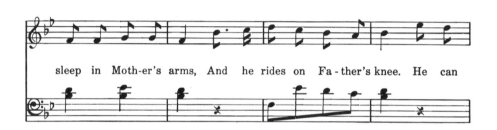

sleep in Moth-er's arms, And he rides on Fa - ther's knee. He can

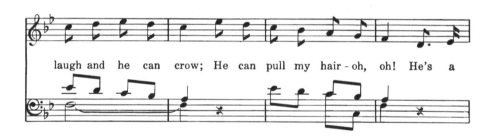

laugh and he can crow; He can pull my hair - oh, oh! He's a

jol - ly boy, ho, ho! And he's ver - y fond of me.

56

Hush-a-by, Baby

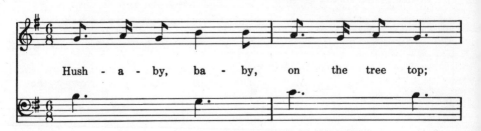

Hush - a - by, ba - by, on the tree top;

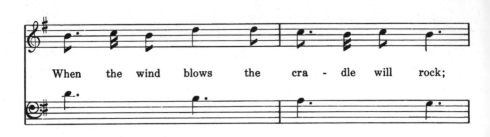

When the wind blows the cra - dle will rock;

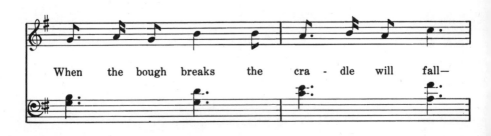

When the bough breaks the cra - dle will fall—

Down will come ba - by, cra - dle and all.

Evening Song

CLARA BELLE BAKER

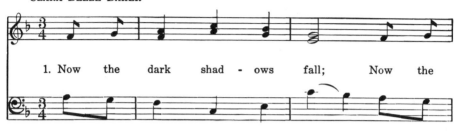

1. Now the dark shad - ows fall; Now the

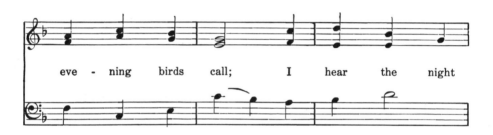

eve - ning birds call; I hear the night

breeze Rus - tle soft through the trees.

2 In my wee bed I lie
While the moon climbs the sky.
I pray you to keep,
Dear Lord, close while I sleep.

Lullaby

CHRISTINA ROSSETTI

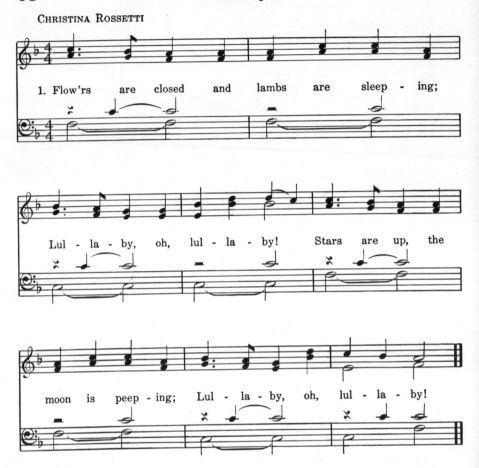

1. Flow'rs are closed and lambs are sleep - ing;

Lul - la - by, oh, lul - la - by! Stars are up, the

moon is peep - ing; Lul - la - by, oh, lul - la - by!

2 While the birds are silence keeping,
Lullaby, oh, lullaby!
Sleep, my baby, fall a-sleeping,
Lullaby, oh, lullaby!

1. Sleep, my child, and peace at - tend thee All through the night.

Guar - dian an - gels God will send thee All through the night.

Soft the drow - sy hours are creep-ing, Hill and vale in slum-ber steep-ing.

I my lov - ing watch am keep-ing All through the night.

2 Mother dear is close beside thee
All through the night,
Watching that no harm betide thee
All through the night.
Through the open window streaming,
Moonlight on the floor is gleaming,
While my baby lies a-dreaming,
All through the night.

EVERY DAY AND SPECIAL DAYS

Tick - tock

CLARA BELLE BAKER

1. Up - on the stair - case land - ing, Tick - tock, tick - tock, Tick-

tock, tick - tock, Up - on the stair - case land - ing There

stands a big hall clock—Tick-tock—There stands a big hall clock.

2 We wake up in the morning,
    Tick-tock, tick-tock,
    Tick-tock, tick-tock,
We wake up in the morning
At sound of that big clock—
    Tick-tock—
At sound of that big clock.

3 We go to kindergarten,
    Tick-tock, tick-tock,
    Tick-tock, tick-tock,
We go to kindergarten,
At bid of that big clock —
    Tick-tock—
At bid of that big clock.

4 We come home to our dinner,
    Tick-tock, tick-tock,
    Tick-tock, tick-tock,
We come home to our dinner
At call of that big clock—
    Tick-tock—
At call of that big clock.

(*Very softly*)

5 At night we go to dreamland,
    Tick-tock, tick-tock,
    Tick-tock, tick-tock,
At night we go to dreamland
By croon of that big clock—
    Tick-tock—
By croon of that big clock.

Good Morning

CLARA BELLE BAKER

Good morn - ing to you, chil - dren dear, Good

morn - ing, we will say. We'll sing and play while

we are here, And have a hap - py day, And

have a hap - py day, And have a hap - py day!

Good-by

CLARA BELLE BAKER

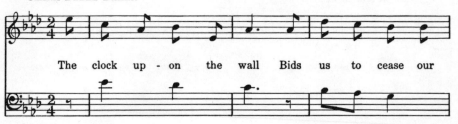

The clock up - on the wall Bids us to cease our

song and play, And come a - gain an - oth - er day. Good-

by, good - by to all, Good - by, good - by to all.

Birthday Candles

Clara Belle Baker

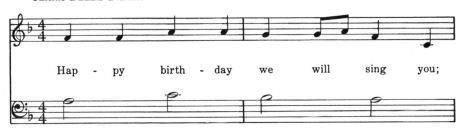

Hap - py birth - day we will sing you;

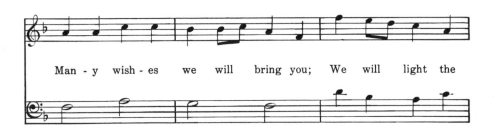

Man - y wish - es we will bring you; We will light the

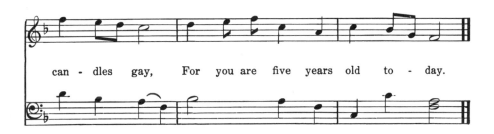

can - dles gay, For you are five years old to - day.

When My Father Goes Away

BERTHA RHODES

When my fa - ther goes a - way,

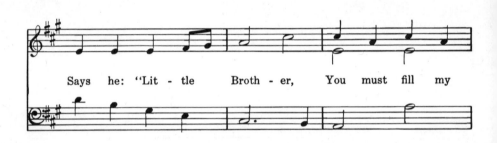

Says he: "Lit - tle Broth - er, You must fill my

place to - day, Take good care of Moth - er."

GABRIEL SETOUN

The world's a ver - y hap - py place, Where

ev - 'ry child should dance and sing, And al - ways show a

smil - ing face, And nev - er sulk for an - y - thing.

68 Happy Thought

ROBERT LOUIS STEVENSON

The world is so full of a num - ber of things, I am
sure we should all be as hap - py as kings.

Glad Thanksgiving Day

CLARA BELLE BAKER

On glad Thanks-giv - ing Day The chil - dren will be

gay. We like the din - ner of tur - key and spice; We

like the can - dies and nuts and ice, And then we like to

play On glad Thanks - giv - ing Day——

The Jack-o'-Lantern

LOIS HOLT

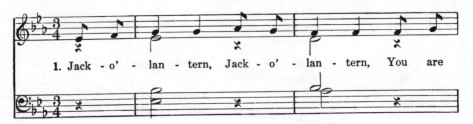

1. Jack - o' - lan - tern, Jack - o' - lan - tern, You are

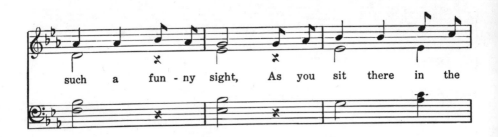

such a fun - ny sight, As you sit there in the

win - dow, Look - ing out at the night.

2 You were once a yellow pumpkin,
  Growing on a sturdy vine;
Now you are a Jack-o'-lantern;
  See the candle-light shine!

Valentines

CLARA BELLE BAKER

When days of Feb-ru-a-ry come I know what I will
do: I'll make some pret-ty val-en-tines of pa-per red and
blue. Tra-la-la! Tra-la-la! Tra-la-la-la-la-la-la-la! Tra-la-
la! Tra-la-la! Tra-la-la-la-la-la-la In
Feb-ru-a-ry I will send a val-en-tine to you.

72   Glad Easter Is Here

CLARA BELLE BAKER

Be of cheer! Glad Eas - ter time is here! The

church bells all are ring - ing, And chil-dren's voi - ces sing - ing!

Be of cheer! Glad Eas - ter time is here!

America

73

SAMUEL FRANCIS SMITH

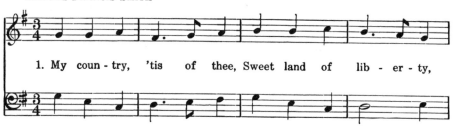

1. My coun - try, 'tis of thee, Sweet land of lib - er - ty,

Of thee I sing. Land where my fa - thers died! Land of the

pil-grims' pride! From ev - 'ry moun-tain side Let free-dom ring!

2 Our fathers' God, to thee,
  Author of liberty,
    To thee we sing.
  Long may our land be bright
  With freedom's holy light;
  Protect us by thy might,
    Great God, our King!

NOTE.—This simplified harmonization of "America" is offered for the use of the child at the piano. For group singing the familiar four-part harmonization is everywhere available.

Christmas Bells

CLARA BELLE BAKER

Christ - mas bells, Christ - mas bells, Ring out clear!

Each one tells Christ - mas time is here.

Christmas Is Coming

CLARA BELLE BAKER

Glad Christ - mas is com - ing, Glad Christ - mas is

near. Old San - ta makes read - y His sleigh and rein - deer.

FINE

And we will whis - per man - y se - crets, But you must not hear!

D. C. al FINE

76 Christmas Tree

CLARA BELLE BAKER

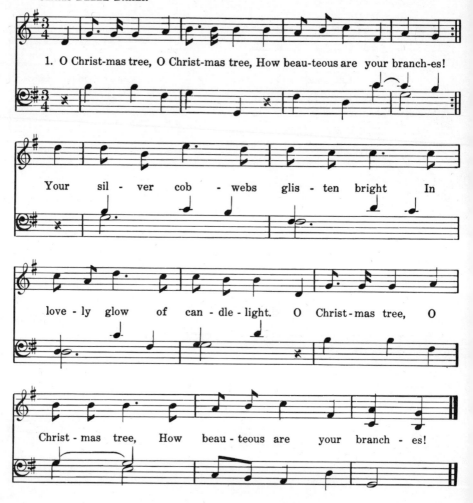

1. O Christ-mas tree, O Christ-mas tree, How beau-teous are your branch-es!

Your sil - ver cob - webs glis - ten bright In

love - ly glow of can - dle - light. O Christ-mas tree, O

Christ - mas tree, How beau - teous are your branch - es!

2 O Christmas tree, O Christmas tree,
How laden are your branches!
High at your top a radiant star
Bids all to come where wonders are.
O Christmas tree, O Christmas tree,
How laden are your branches!

THE CHILD'S WORSHIP

78 Silent Night

1. Si - lent night, ho - ly night, All is calm, all is bright Round yon Vir - gin Moth - er and Child, Ho - ly In - fant so ten - der and mild; Sleep in heav - en - ly peace, Sleep in heav - en - ly peace.

2 Silent night, holy night,
   Shepherds quake at the sight;
   Glories stream from heaven afar,
   Heavenly hosts sing Alleluia;
   Christ the Saviour is born,
   Christ the Saviour is born.

There Came a Child From Heaven 79

MARTIN LUTHER

There came a Child from heav'n a - bove, To
bring us words of joy and love. A
bless - ed mes - sage he did bring, Of
which to - day we speak and sing.

80 Away in a Manger

MARTIN LUTHER   MARTIN LUTHER

1. A - way in a man - ger, No crib for his bed, The
lit - tle Lord Je - sus Laid down his sweet head. The
stars in the heav - ens Looked down where he lay, The
lit - tle Lord Je - sus, A - sleep on the hay.

2 The cattle are lowing;
    The baby awakes;
But little Lord Jesus,
    No crying he makes.
I love thee, Lord Jesus;
    Look down from the sky,
And stay by my cradle
    Till morning is nigh.

A Christmas Lullaby

JESSIE WINTER

Sleep, Ba - by, sleep. Their watch the shep - herds

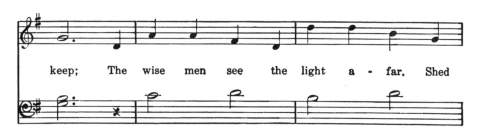

keep; The wise men see the light a - far. Shed

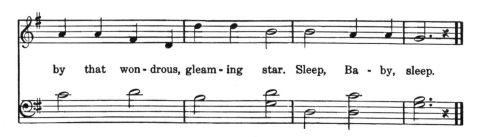

by that won - drous, gleam - ing star. Sleep, Ba - by, sleep.

The Child Jesus

EDNA DEAN BAKER

The dear lit-tle Je-sus once lay on the hay: He
slept and he smiled and he grew day by day Un-
til he could run and could play and could be A
help to his moth-er, like you and like me.

Jesus and the Children

CLARA BELLE BAKER

When Je-sus was on earth with men, He called the lit - tle chil-dren; The

moth-ers heard and glad - ly then They brought the lit - tle chil-dren. He

took them in his arms of love And told a - bout the

Rit.

God a - bove, Who cares for lit - tle chil - dren.

84 All Things Bright and Beautiful

CECIL F. ALEXANDER

1. All things bright and beau - ti - ful, All crea - tures great and small, All things wise and won - der - ful, The Lord God made them all.

2 Each little flower that opens,
Each little bird that sings,
He made their glowing colors,
He made their tiny wings.

3 The cold wind in the winter,
The pleasant summer sun,
The ripe fruits in the garden,
He made them every one.

4 He gave us eyes to see them,
And lips that we might tell
How great is God Almighty
Who has made all things well.

*Small notes for verses 2, 3 and 4.

God Loves Me

EDNA DEAN BAKER

Lit - tle bird and flower and bee, Tell me that God loves me. Sun and wind and rain, all three,

Tell me that God loves me. Moon and stars at night I see, Tell me that God loves me.

God is Good

REINECKE

God is great, and God is good; Him we thank for dai - ly food. By his boun - ty we are fed; By his love we all are led.

We Thank Thee, Loving Father

87

H. GERMAN

We thank thee, lov - ing Fa - ther, For all thy ten - der care, For food and clothes and shel - ter And all thy world so fair

Evening Prayer

MARY LUNDIE DUNCAN (Adapted)

1. Heav'n-ly Fa - ther, wilt thou hear me?
Bless thy lit - tle child to - night;
Through the dark - ness be thou near me;
Keep me safe till morn - ing light.

2 All this day thy hand has led me;
And I thank thee for thy care;
Thou hast clothed me, warmed, and fed me;
Listen to my evening prayer.

Now I Wake

New England Primer (Adapted)

From SCHUMANN

Now I wake and see the light;

God has kept me through the night; —

I will lift my eyes and pray:

Keep me, Fa - ther, through the day.

90 Praise Him

CLARA BELLE BAKER

For rain and sun - shine and flow - ers bright and fair,

Fa - ther and moth - er who give us lov - ing care,

Praise him, praise him, praise him, our God.

Sing, lit - tle chil - dren, oh! sing ev - 'ry - where.